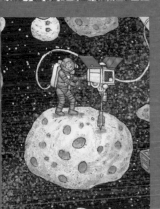

SECRET SQUID GOES TO SPACE

Illustrated by Barry Ablett

CONTENTS

INTRODUCTION

Meet Secret Squid, a master of disguise who can be in lots of different places at once! With a talent for hiding in plain sight, Squid is able to get into all sorts of mischief without being discovered.

SECRET MISSION

Join Secret Squid on a sneaky mission to uncover the secrets and remarkable wonders of space. From preparing to launch to the possibility of living on the Moon, our tentacled friend is ready to buckle up, explore and have lots of fun!

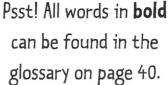

Psst! All words in **bold** can be found in the glossary on page 40.

THE SEARCH IS ON

Can you find all of Secret Squid's hiding places? Our sneaky friend has snuck into 10 different locations in each scene, wearing some very clever disguises. While you are searching, don't forget to check out your surroundings. There's a lot to spot while journeying through space!

Having trouble finding me? All my hiding places are revealed on pages 38–39.

THE JOURNEY CONTINUES

Turn the page after each scene to discover more about each experience and the wonders of space.

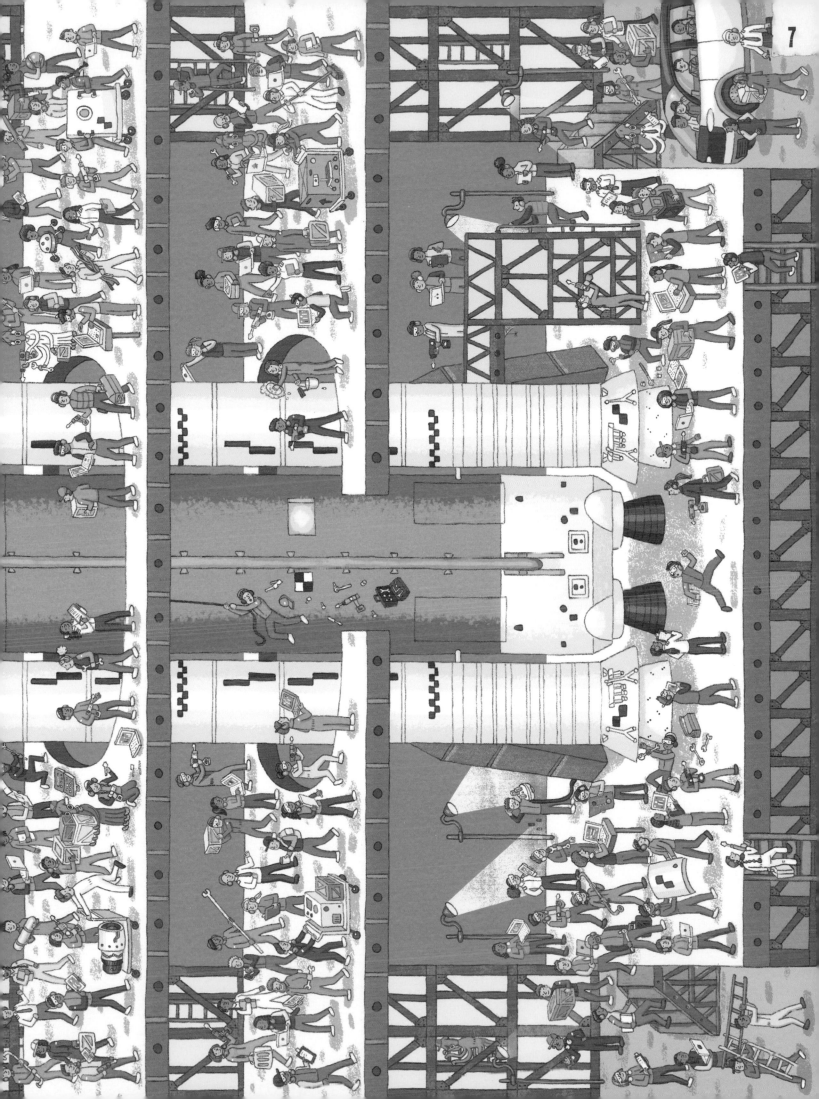

THE LAUNCH

When it comes to exploring space, there is lots of preparation to do here on Earth! This includes making sure the rocket is ready for its launch into space. But how does a rocket get off the ground in the first place?

THE CREW

These are the people that get to explore space! They travel up into space inside the rocket and are known as **astronauts.**

WELCOME TO THE LAUNCH PAD

The launch pad is the platform that the rocket blasts off from. It allows the rocket to launch safely from a stable surface, as well as makes it easy for **engineers** to fix any problems the rocket may have.

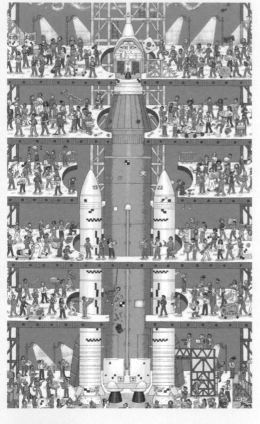

TEAMWORK

The rocket wouldn't launch without the teamwork of everybody on the ground. Lots of people work together to ensure the rocket is safe and ready for its mission.

ORION

Orion is a new spacecraft created by **NASA**. It has been built to explore space in a way that hasn't been done before, allowing deeper travel into space and a safe return back to Earth.

LAUNCH ABORT SYSTEM

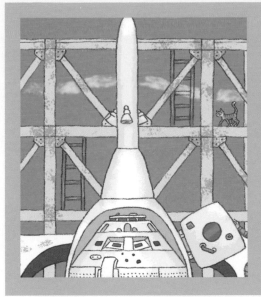

The launch abort system is at the top of this rocket. In case of an emergency when launching, this section is designed to carry the crew back to safety.

BIG BOOST

Boosters are rocket engines that are attached to the main spacecraft. They give the rocket extra power during its launch. The boosters fall back to Earth once all the fuel has been used.

RS-25 ENGINES

So what gets this rocket off the ground? RS-25 engines are the main engines attached to the spacecraft. They have completed many missions and continue to be one of the most tested rocket engines in the world.

CREW MODULE

The crew module is where the crew stays during their journey into space. Astronauts live and work in this small space for up to six months.

PUBLIC AFFAIRS

PROPULSION

GUIDANCE NAVIGATION AND CONTROL

COMMAND AND DATA

FLIGHT DYNAMICS

INTEGRATED COMMUNICATIONS

FLIGHT

FLIGHT OPERATIONS

FLIGHT OPERATIONS

MISSION CONTROL

So, the rocket launch has been successful and the astronauts are beginning their journey into space, but what happens down on the ground? Who keeps an eye out for the rocket and the crew on board? Let's look into what happens in a mission control room.

ROCKET LAUNCH

Mission control keeps a close eye on the rocket, showing the launch on a big screen for everybody to watch. This allows the team to watch the takeoff and celebrate the successful mission!

GROUND TEAM

The ground team is a large group that plans and carries out the mission, watching the rocket on its journey. The ground officer oversees the spacecraft mission and makes sure everything is running smoothly and safely.

WORKING HARD

It is very important to have people checking on the whereabouts and the status of the rocket at all times. That's why mission control is open 24/7. The spacecraft mission relies on the team on the ground to make sure everything runs smoothly and that the crew returns safely to Earth. There are always staff on duty, working hard!

ENGINEERS

From the mission control room, engineers carry out checks on the spacecraft during its long journey. They can also communicate in real time with the crew in case any problems occur.

SPACE COMMUNICATION

As well as helping with the rocket launch, mission control keeps in contact with the crew on the spacecraft during their long journey. Can you imagine calling somebody who's in space?

FLIGHT TEAM

The flight team is responsible for planning the route in which the rocket takes. They ensure the mission is a success and the rocket can return to Earth safely and without any problems.

TIME-OUT

With everybody working so hard on the ground, it is important for them to take a break! Staff members bring around food and water to make sure everybody can focus and do the best job they can.

KEEPING TRACK

Without mission control, there would be no rocket launch! They may not be as celebrated as astronauts are, but they are just as important, and are one of the reasons we can explore space successfully!

ON THE MOON

Earth's rocky, cratered Moon is the only place beyond Earth where humans have set foot...so far! But one day in the near future, humans may live and work on the Moon, and use it as a base for faraway space travel.

GROWING FOOD

There aren't any plants growing on the Moon yet; the conditions are too harsh. Like humans, plants need plenty of oxygen and water to survive. Scientists will need to build giant **greenhouses** to grow food in outer space or else they'll be very hungry!

SUPER SPACESUITS

Astronauts couldn't survive without their spacesuits! The suits protect them from the extreme temperatures of space, and provide **oxygen** to breathe.

WHAT ABOUT WATER?

The Moon doesn't have many lakes or rivers like Earth, so scientists are thinking about clever ways to find water. Maybe they will find ways to bring water from Earth or use ice found on the Moon.

A LONG DAY

Did you know that one day on the Moon lasts for 328 hours? That means lots of sunlight for solar panels to turn into electricity!

WHAT'S BELOW?

Below the surface, there may be useful materials that lead to the creation of fuel and water, or construction materials, like metal. If astronauts can use natural materials they find on the Moon, they won't have to rely as much on deliveries from Earth!

RECORD-BREAKING RESEARCH

The Moon is the first step on humankind's journey to Mars in **NASA's Artemis mission**. As well as preparing for Mars, scientists will experiment on the Moon's soil and rocks to learn its secrets and explore the areas that never get any sunlight!

FIRST PEOPLE ON THE MOON

In 1969, humans walked on the Moon for the first time ever! There's no wind or rain on the Moon, which means the first astronauts' footsteps will be there for years.

FLOATING IN SPACE

Despite there being some **gravity** on the Moon, it is nothing compared to gravity here on Earth! If you were to walk around on the Moon, you would have to make sure you were attached to your spacecraft. If not, you might float off into space!

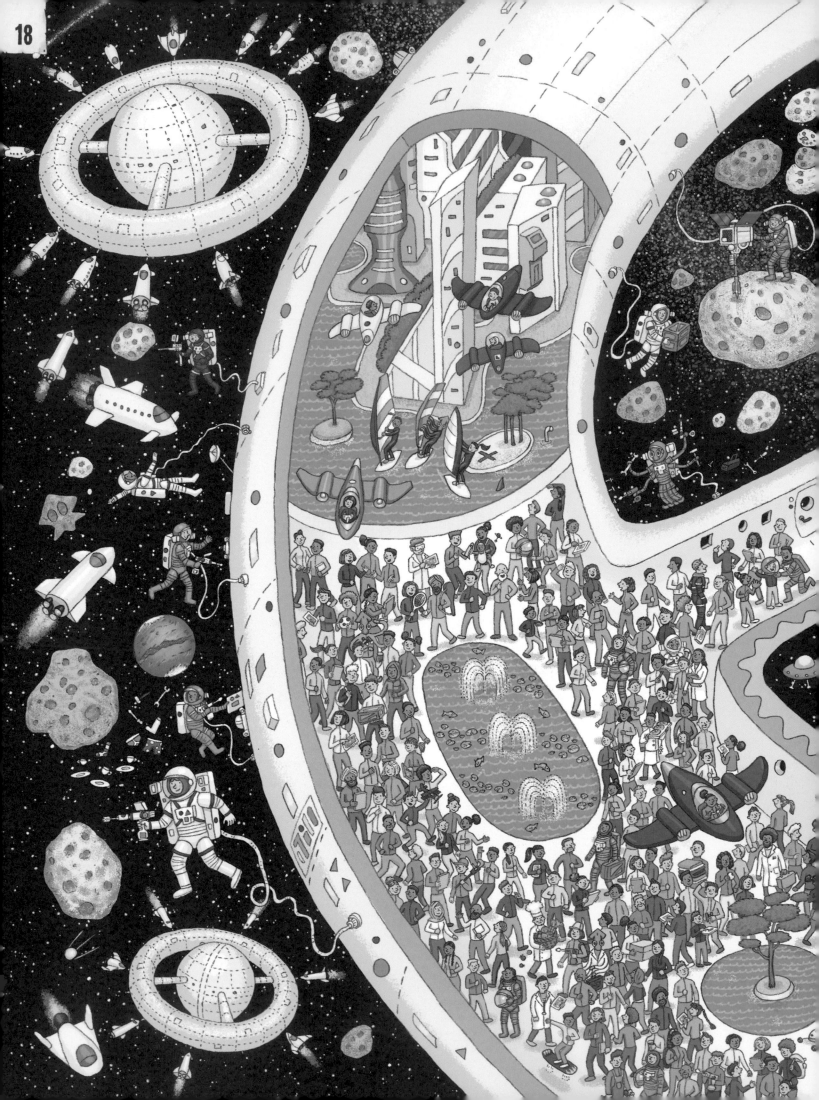

SPACE COLONY

Imagine looking out of the window every day and all you can see is space! This is what life would be like in a space colony. Scientists are currently researching if it's possible for us to live so far from Earth. Can you imagine living on a space station?

CREATING GRAVITY

To create the feeling of gravity, a space station would need to be constantly rotating to copy our planet Earth!

EXTRA-TERRESTRIAL EXERCISE

Would you like to go for a run in the sky? Doing exercise would be essential for anybody living in outer space. Our bodies would not be used to zero gravity, so staying as fit and healthy as possible would be very important.

NEED A JOB?

Adapting to life in space would create lots of new, exciting jobs. These might include space pilots, space farmers and, of course, astronauts! Would you feel like working up in the galaxy?

SPACE SLEEP

Sleeping in space would be a strange feeling, especially with no gravity! Precautions would have to be made, such as tying sleeping bags to a wall when going to bed to avoid floating away!

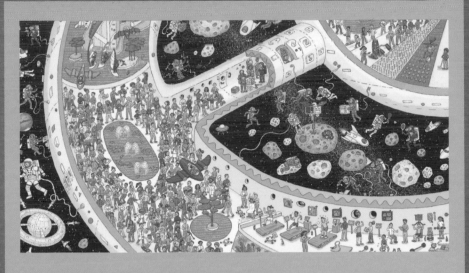

AMAZING ARCHITECTURE

So what would a space station look like? The current model looks like a large circular section, surrounded by a wheel-like structure that slowly spins.

MINING

For humans to live in space long-term, we would need to have access to water, food and oxygen. This could involve **mining** the surface of nearby planets in order to find all the essentials we need to live.

STEPPING OUT INTO SPACE

One of the most exciting parts of living in space is that you could explore a completely new place! Would you be brave enough to suit up and step out into the stars? Where would you want to explore first?

HAVING FUN!

As fun as it would be to live in space, we might want to bring some things from Earth to keep us entertained, too!

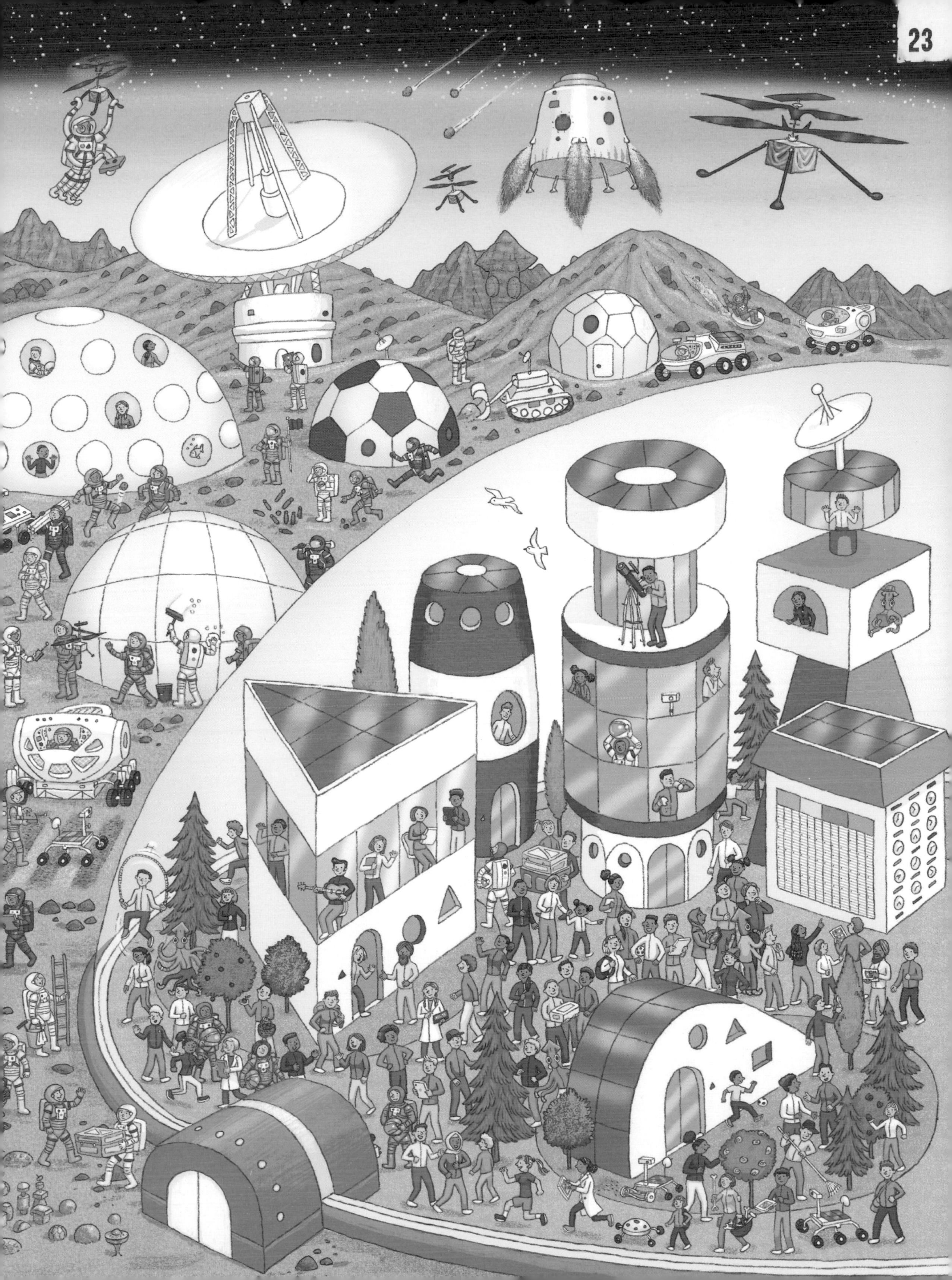

LIVING ON MARS

Have you ever wondered if humans can live on Mars? It may seem very far away, but living on the Red Planet isn't just a dream. Scientists and engineers are working hard to make it happen! Let's explore what living on Mars would be like...

GREAT VIEWS

One great thing about living on Mars would be just how much you could see. There would be plenty of star-gazing for the people living there. Imagine looking out to space with a telescope and being able to see Earth!

LONG-DISTANCE CALLS

Would you like to make a call from space? Thanks to special **satellite** dishes, scientists believe that communication between Earth and Mars would be possible.

GREEN SPACE

Being surrounded by nature would be just as important for humans on Mars as it is for humans on Earth! Connecting with nature makes us feel good, and creates clean air for us to breathe. Filling biodomes with trees would be very important for surviving on Mars.

BIODOME SAFETY

If we were to survive on Mars, we would need to stay under **biodome** roofs to keep safe. These big enclosed domes would imitate Earth-like conditions, creating an environment that humans could survive in for a long amount of time, not just for a visit!

ROVERS AND LANDERS

Rovers are small vehicles that move around the surface of planets. There are currently many rovers exploring Mars! Scientists can control the movements of rovers all the way from Earth. How impressive is that?

GETTING AROUND

How exactly would we get around if humans lived on Mars? Scientists would have to build special vehicles to ensure safe human travel. Mars is much colder than here on Earth, so a heater built into the vehicles would be essential!

A LONG YEAR

Did you know that Mars has longer years than Earth? There are 687 Earth days in just one Mars year! A day there is also 40 minutes longer. Think of all the extra fun you could have on Mars!

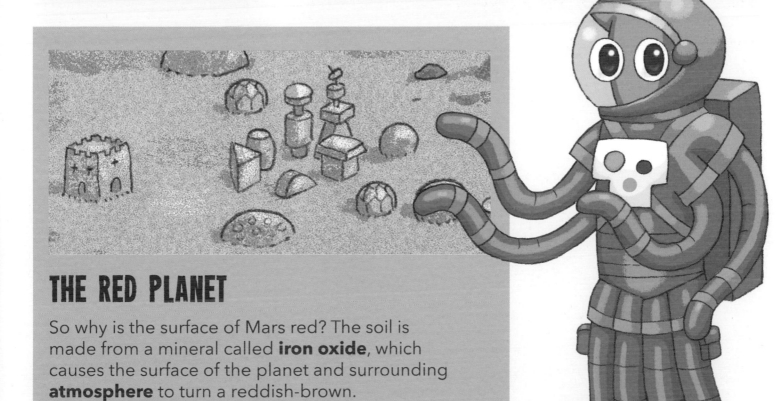

THE RED PLANET

So why is the surface of Mars red? The soil is made from a mineral called **iron oxide**, which causes the surface of the planet and surrounding **atmosphere** to turn a reddish-brown.

ALIEN ENCOUNTER

It's difficult to know exactly what an alien might look like, or what different shapes and sizes they might be. Scientists have come up with lots of ideas, based on the types of planets they could be found on and how they might live...

THE GREEN ONES

When we think of what aliens might look like, what comes to mind? Green creatures with big heads? Lots of tentacle-shaped legs? One giant eye? This may be the most common idea of what an alien could look like, but let's explore some more…

BREATHING BUBBLES

How might an alien breathe in space? Some scientists imagine that aliens would make an oxygen bag around themselves to stay alive!

SPECTACULAR SPACESHIPS

It's interesting to think about how an alien might **inhabit** a planet. Would they simply exist on the surface or could they build somewhere to live, like we do? Maybe they would live in a huge spaceship, like this one!

FLYING OR FLOATING?

It's possible that some aliens could be like birds and have wings! But would they fly or would they float through space? Perhaps their large wingspans would be used to float on the breeze.

MUSHROOM OR ALIEN?

Aliens could look like things we have on Earth – like plants or animals! Some scientists imagine aliens could look like large mushrooms, but with lots of tentacles under their bodies!

DINOSAUR LOOK-ALIKES

When you think of aliens, do you think of dinosaurs? Some scientists do! They believe some aliens could have a dinosaur-shaped body and a long snout for sucking up water.

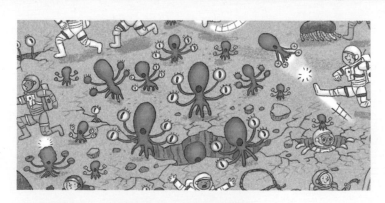

LIVING UNDERGROUND

If aliens do exist, where do you think they might live? Some scientists believe that aliens would burrow underground, just like moles and rabbits do on Earth! What do you think about this?

ALIEN HUNTING HABITS

Aliens would have to be well adapted to hunt in outer space, which could mean clever methods and unusual body parts. Some scientists believe that aliens would extend their long tongues to find and catch food. Weird!

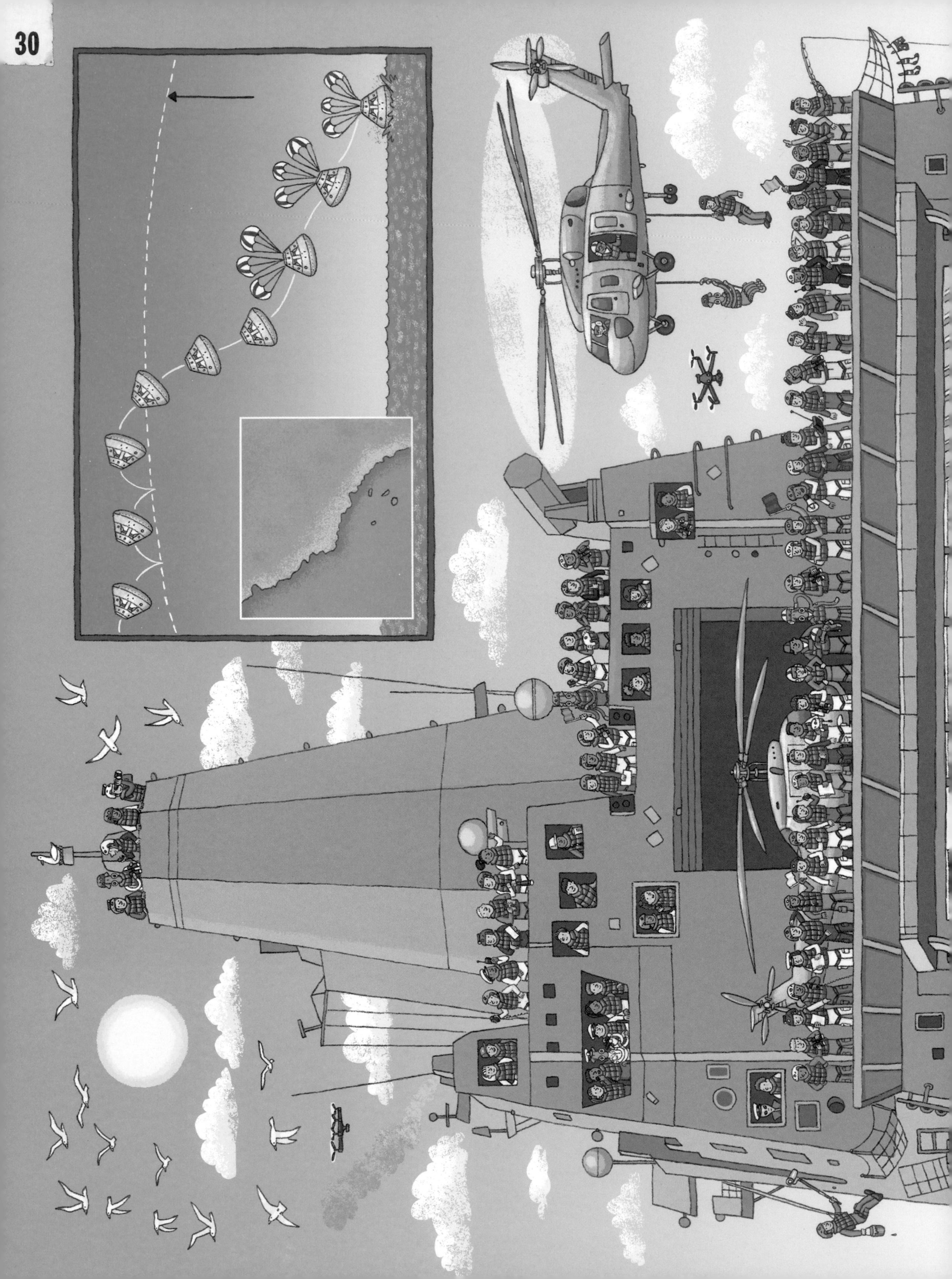

SPLASH DOWN

After the spacecraft has finished its amazing journey through space, how does it return back to Earth? It's likely you have seen a rocket launch into space, but have you ever seen a rocket land back down?

SPEEDY SPACECRAFT

When it comes to returning to the Earth's **orbit**, a rocket will put its engines back on and fly backward to decrease its speed! When the rocket reenters the Earth's atmosphere, gravity pulls the spacecraft back to Earth for landing.

...AND SPLASH!

When a spacecraft returns from a mission, it doesn't return back to where it set off. Instead, most spacecrafts land gently down into the ocean. This is the safest way to bring a rocket back to Earth. It's not only safer for the crew, but also avoids the risk of damaging areas of land.

TIME TO PARACHUTE

To make sure the returning rocket has a safe landing, parachutes are needed to slow the rocket down to a safe speed before the spacecraft hits the water.

HEATED PROTECTION

A heat shield helps a rocket slow down as it reenters the Earth's atmosphere. It is made up of **carbon-carbon tiles** that are located on the nose of the rocket.

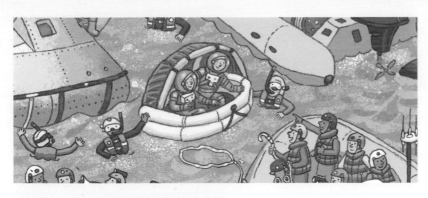

THE CREW RETURNS

Once the rocket has landed safely, the crew leaves the spacecraft and enters the water. They are collected in lifeboats that are waiting ready for their arrival. Can you imagine how you'd feel after a flight all the way from outer space? You'd definitely want to stretch your legs!

WELCOME HOME

When the rocket is due to return to Earth, many people come to watch and celebrate. This includes family and friends of the crew, people who worked on the mission and any space lovers!

INSPECTIONS, PLEASE!

When the crew reaches the lifeboats, each member is thoroughly inspected by medics to ensure they are in good shape after their long journey to and from space.

BACK TO SHORE

After making sure the crew is safe, the team travels back to shore in a large ship as the final part of their mission. Once the crew has taken time to rest, they return to mission control to let the team know what they discovered in space!

DID YOU SPOT...

Here are some interesting characters and items that you may have missed. Head back to each scene to see if you can find them!

...FLOATING TOOLS

In 2023, a NASA astronaut was completing checks on the **International Space Station** when his tool bag floated away into space! It now orbits Earth and can sometimes be spotted in the sky from Earth!

Find on pages 18–19

...CHEESY MOON

Despite scientists confirming the theory to be untrue, a **medieval** tale told the story of our Moon being made out of cheese, and many people believed this tale until space exploration in the 1960s!

Find on pages 14–15

...ICY METEORITE

In 1982, a **meteorite** was discovered by scientists in Antarctica. After lots of research, they found out this meteorite had flown all the way from the Moon! Since then, many meteorites from the Moon have been found on Earth.

Find on pages 18–19

...LANDERS AND ROVERS

A lander is a small spacecraft that lands on the surface of a planet. A rover is taken inside a lander to a planet, and they both explore the surface, taking pictures and collecting information as they go. Both landers and rovers carry out important experiments for scientists to learn about other planets.

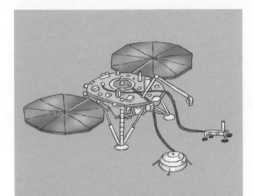

INSIGHT LANDER

In 2018, the InSight lander was the first robot to explore under the surface of Mars. It was able to go deep under the surface, discovering how Mars formed, the temperature of the planet and how meteorites impact the planet's structure.

Find on pages 22-23

INGENUITY HELICOPTER

The Ingenuity helicopter, also nicknamed Ginny, is a helicopter that operates on Mars. This was the first aircraft to accomplish controlled and powered flight on a different planet. It was part of NASA's 2020 mission to the Red Planet.

Find on pages 22-23

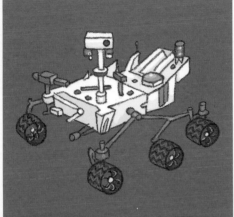

CURIOSITY ROVER

In 2012, the Curiosity rover arrived on Mars. This is the largest, most advanced rover sent to space so far. It picks up soil and rocks from the planet's surface and takes them back on board for further research. This helps scientists on Earth learn about the history and formation of Mars.

Find on pages 22-23

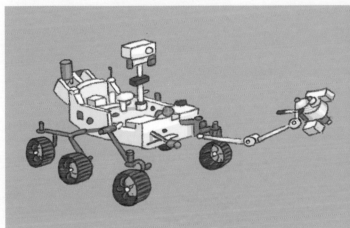

PERSEVERANCE ROVER

Alongside the Ingenuity helicopter, the Perseverance rover set off for Mars in 2020. This vehicle explores the surface of the Red Planet for signs of ancient life. It is always on the lookout for signs of new life too!

Find on pages 22-23

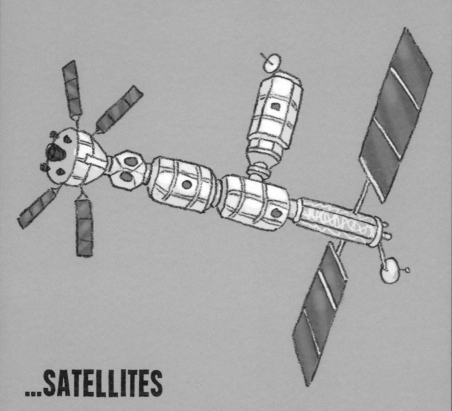

...SATELLITES

A satellite is a type of spacecraft that orbits a planet or star. It takes photos of our universe, helps other spacecraft navigate and allows scientists understand our planet from afar!

Find on pages 14-15

...WEATHER FORECASTING

Did you know that you can spot tornadoes and hurricanes on Earth from space? Scientists use satellites to predict future weather patterns.

Find on pages 14-15

...COMMUNITIES

Community matters! Spending time with friends and family would be an important part of adjusting to life in outer space. Imagine playing sports with a friend...while floating around!

Find on pages 18-19

...SOLAR SYSTEM SCIENCE

Think how much more we could learn about space...in space! By living on the Moon or Mars, scientists would make exciting new discoveries all the time, helping us learn more about the solar system than ever before.

Find on pages 14–15

...HOBBIES

Keeping up with activities you enjoy is important when you move anywhere new. Space is no exception! What are some hobbies that you enjoy taking part in?

Find on pages 22–23

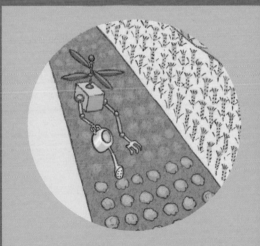

...MACHINES AT WORK

If humans were to live in a space colony, there would need to be new technology to help us. Maybe there could be special robots to help grow, water and collect crops for humans to turn into yummy food...

Find on pages 18–19

...A PET ALIEN

If there really is alien life out there, do you think they would be friends or **foes**? Or do you think we might keep some as pets?

Find on pages 26–27

ANSWERS

Did you manage to find all of
Secret Squid's hiding places?

MISSION CONTROL Pages 10-11

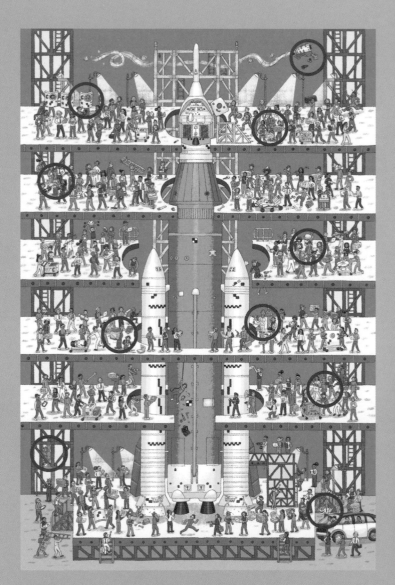

THE LAUNCH Pages 6-7

ON THE MOON Pages 14-15

SPACE COLONY Pages 18-19

LIVING ON MARS Pages 22-23

ALIEN ENCOUNTER Pages 26-27

Check the circles on these pictures to reveal my secret locations.

SPLASH DOWN Pages 30-31

GLOSSARY

adapting – changing to fit a new environment or situation.

astronauts – scientists that travel to space on a spaceship. *Astronaut* comes from the Greek word meaning "space sailor".

atmosphere – the area surrounding a planet, made up of layers of gas.

biodome – a self-contained space created by humans to live in.

carbon-carbon tiles – strong shields used on spaceships that keep them protected from hot areas in the atmosphere (see above).

engineers – people who design and build complex structures, such as buildings and machines.

foes – enemies.

gravity – an invisible force that pulls things toward each other. This is how humans stay on Earth!

greenhouses – glass buildings used to grow flowers and vegetables.

inhabit – to live in.

International Space Station – a large spacecraft that orbits (see right) Earth. It is where astronauts (see left) live when they are in space.

iron oxide – a type of red powder found in the soil on Mars that is made up of iron and oxygen (see right).

medieval – a time period in Europe that began in approximately 500 CE and lasted around 1,000 years.

meteorite – a rock that falls to Earth from space.

mining – searching and taking out useful materials from the ground.

NASA – a US agency that is responsible for space science and technology. NASA stands for National Aeronautics and Space Administration.

NASA Artemis mission – a mission carried out by NASA (see above) to explore the surface of the Moon.

orbit – to repeatedly travel around a planet, moon or a star.

oxygen – a gas that is necessary for plants and animals to survive.

satellite – any object that orbits a planet. It can be a natural or man-made item.

First published in 2024 by Hungry Tomato Ltd.
F15, Old Bakery Studios, Blewetts Wharf, Malpas Road, Truro, Cornwall, TR1 1QH, UK

Thanks to our creative team:
Editor: Millie Burdett
Editor: Holly Thornton
Senior Graphic Designer: Amy Harvey

Beetle Books is an imprint of Hungry Tomato.

ISBN 9781916598638

Printed and bound in China.

A CIP catalog record for this book is available from the British Library.

Discover more at:
www.mybeetlebooks.com
www.hungrytomato.com